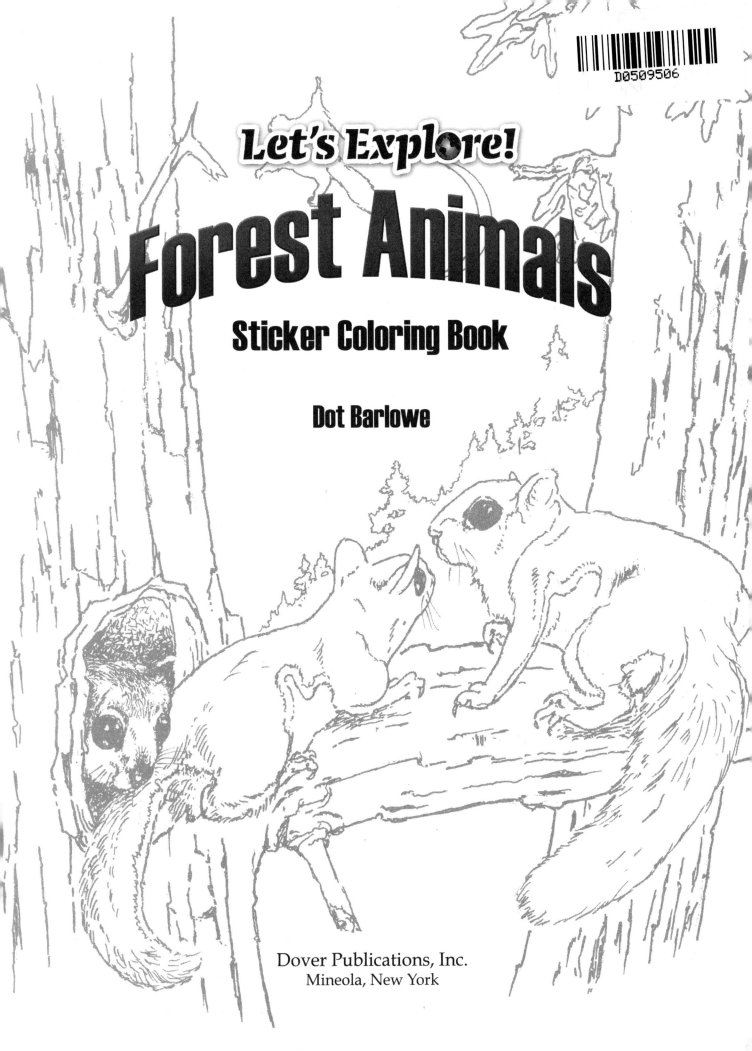

Let's Explore!

Forest Animals

Sticker Coloring Book

Dot Barlowe

Dover Publications, Inc.
Mineola, New York

NOTE

You probably know that forests are large areas covered in trees and plants. But what about the animals that live in these regions? All forests have a changing climate that goes through all four seasons — spring, summer, fall, and winter — and forest animals have had to adapt to both the heat and the cold. Thousands of animal species live in the forest. There are small animals like the rabbit, and big animals like the brown bear. Depending on what part of the world you're in, you might find woodchucks, turkeys, raccoons, bobcats, coyotes, and others. You can learn about all these and more inside this book, where an exciting forest adventure is waiting for you! Educational and fun, this coloring collection features thirty accurately rendered illustrations of forest animals to color, interesting fact-filled captions, plus 31 stickers — each of which will fit into a gray outline on the appropriate coloring page.

Bibliographical Note

Let's Explore! Forest Animals Sticker Coloring Book is a new work, first published by Dover Publications, Inc., in 2011.

International Standard Book Number

ISBN-13: 978-0-486-47894-4
ISBN-10: 0-486-47894-7

Manufactured in the United States by RR Donnelley
47894703   2015
www.doverpublications.com

Found all the continents except Antarctica and Australia, the mouse-like **shrew** is very territorial, and will viciously defend its territory from rivals. Most dig burrows under dirt or snow in order to surprise their prey.

Although the **flying squirrel** cannot actually fly, the parachute-like flap of skin between their wrists and ankles allows them to glide through the air for long distances. The flying squirrel is known to be very noisy, and chatters for long periods of time.

The **blue jay** is one of the most common birds in the United States. It can make a large variety of sounds, usually mimicking the calls of other birds. The *mink* can be found near or in bodies of water. It is usually alone, and will defend its territory if another mink intrudes.

Despite its name, the **red squirrel** can be found in any shade from orange-brown to almost black. It usually lives in a nest made out of twigs, moss, and bark. The *red-shouldered hawk* catches its prey by waiting quietly in a tree and swooping down on a small rodent passing underneath.

The male **pheasant** is easily recognized with its brightly colored feathers and long tail, while the female is tan or brown with a short tail. Baby pheasants look like their mothers until they are about 10 weeks old, when the males begin to grow brighter feathers.

Raccoons usually live together in small groups of three or four, although they hunt or forage for food alone. They are known for their almost human-like "hands," which they use to examine their food before eating it. Unlike most songbirds, the *cardinal* doesn't migrate in the winter, but has adapted to survive the cold eating mostly seeds and winter berries.

Opossums spend a good portion of their time up in the trees, and baby opossums can be spotted hanging upside-down from the trees by their tails. If an opossum feels threatened by a predator, it will fall down and "play dead."

7

Surprisingly, wild **rabbits** often build their nests right in the middle of open fields or meadows. Predators are usually afraid to enter wide open areas, so this works as protection for the baby rabbits.

8

The **deer** is one of the most widely distributed forest animals, found on all the continents except Antarctica and Australia. Deer are most active at dawn and dusk, usually resting during the midday hours.

9

Red foxes usually travel together in small groups of 6 to 8, with one male and one female being designated the "leaders." When the female "leader" has *kits* (baby foxes) all the foxes in the group help raise them.

Gray squirrels spend most of their lives in trees, and generally live in the same place year round. They have very good balance, and can jump long distances onto narrow tree branches, and run down tree trunks head first without falling.

One of the largest species of mammal in North America, the **American elk** has the largest antlers of all the deer species combined. Male elks will often antler wrestle in order to gain the attention of a female.

Because the **striped skunk's** stubby legs cause it to be very slow moving, it defends itself from predators by spraying them with a terrible smelling fluid. This confuses the predator, giving the skunk time to get away.

The small, nocturnal *screech owl* is named for its long, loud, and piercing call. The screech owl hunts its prey while perched up in a tree, using its highly developed hearing to listen for rodents like the **deer mouse** pictured here.

Page 27

Page 15

Page 5

Page 4

Page 16

Page 16

Page 1

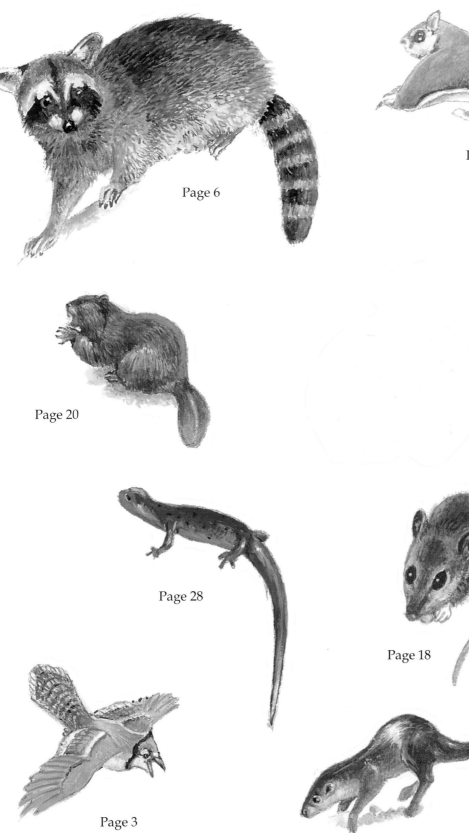

Page 6

Page 2

Page 20

Page 21

Page 28

Page 18

Page 3

Page 19

Page 23

Page 24

Page 11

Page 10

Page 22

Page 25

Page 9

The **wood duck** lays its eggs high up in a tree. When the ducklings are born, they can't fly yet, but must jump down from the tree in order to reach their mother. The ducklings can fall lengths of more than 250 feet without getting hurt!

The **bullfrog** usually lives near larger fresh water bodies, and will feed on nearly any insect, animal, or fish that it can catch. The **green heron** can also be found near fresh water bodies. When hunting, the green heron will usually drop a worm or other insect into the water in order to lure a fish close to the surface. When the fish approaches the bait, the heron swoops down and grabs it.

A medium-sized wild cat, the **bobcat** hunts by stalking its prey and then pouncing on it. It usually eats rabbits and small mammals, and occasionally hunts bigger prey in the winter when its regular food is scarce.

Deer mice are usually gray or brown, with white bellies and feet. They are nocturnal, and do not hibernate during the winter. In wintertime they usually build a nest inside a log or pile of branches, venturing out in order to search for food.

Otters have webbed paws, and spend a lot of their time in the water. They have a special layer of "underfur," which is kept from getting wet by the longer fur on the outside. This acts as insulation, keeping the otter warm—even in very cold water.

19

Beavers like to live on the banks of rivers and lakes, and build dome-shaped "houses" out of sticks, branches and mud. Often, beavers that live near a smaller body of water will make it bigger by gnawing down trees and using the branches to construct a dam.

Pumas are solitary animals, spending most of their lives alone, except for breeding purposes, and mother pumas will live with their kittens for the first two years of their lives. They usually eat larger mammals like deer and elk.

The **groundhog** digs deep burrows for sleeping, hibernating, and storing food. They are very territorial, and will defend the burrow with their long claws and sharp teeth. Groundhogs can be noisy, making a sound similar to a dog's bark, or squealing when antagonized by a predator.

With a coat covered in sharp spines, the **porcupine** is generally protected from predators, though it is occasionally eaten by large birds and snakes. Because of its large, rounded shape, the porcupine is a very slow moving mammal.

One of the most common bats in North America, the **little brown bat** weighs only about 0.5 ounces. It is nocturnal and eats insects. During the winter, little brown bats hibernate in large groups inside of caves.

Coyotes travel together in groups, and generally hunt in pairs. They sleep in burrows that they can dig themselves, but more often steal from groundhogs or other animals. Coyotes will eat any type of animal they can catch.

The bulky **wild turkey** can have up to 6,000 feathers on its body, and can weigh as much as 25 pounds. Despite their size, wild turkeys are good fliers, and will flee at any sign of danger. They eat nuts, berries, and insects.

The **red-headed woodpecker** is known for storing food in holes that it pecks in tree trunks, and in between crevasses in bark. It keeps other birds out of its territory by destroying their nests. The *nuthatch* is a gray or blue bird that eats mostly insects. It has been nicknamed the "upside-down bird" for the way it hangs upside-down by its feet from tree branches.

The *box turtle* has a large, dome-shaped shell, which can be closed completely when the turtle pulls itself inside. This helps to keep it safe from predators. **Eastern newts** usually live in a moist environment either near or in a body of water. They eat insects, worms, and frog eggs.

Chipmunks eat fruit, berries, nuts, insects, and bird eggs. They have pouches in their cheeks in order to carry large amounts of food back to their burrows, where they store it for the wintertime.

Despite it's size, the **brown bear,** which weighs as much as 2,000 pounds, eats mostly fruit, roots, and fish. They also eat insects, especially moths. In the warmer months, the brown bear will eat enough to gain about 400 pounds before it hibernates for the winter.